STEAMTEAM 5 ™

LESSON PLANS

GRADES K-5 VOLUME I

Experiment Disclaimer:

All experiments in these lesson plans have been provided as a resource for teachers, parents and students.

While all due care has been taken, we recommend that an adult supervise children at all times when experiments are performed. Experiments are not recommended for children 3 years and under due to potential choking hazard. Monsoon Publishing LLC does not accept any liability for events that occur as a result of the activities described.

Contents

Introduction

Our mission is to make learning about science, technology, engineering, art, and mathematics fun for kids. We started a publishing company to write and launch the STEAMTEAM 5 adventure book series so that parents and educators everywhere can inspire their kids with great STEM/STEAM role models.

Our first book, "STEAMTEAM 5: The Beginning," is an adventure book about five amazing girls who use science, technology, engineering, art, and math to do amazing things. This book is the first volume of a fictional universe built around five characters: Sandia Scientist, Treeka Technologist, Evelyn Engineer, Ariana Artist, and Mattie Mathematician.

In "STEAMTEAM 5: The Beginning," the newly formed STEAMTEAM 5 embarks on an unexpected adventure after Mattie's beloved dog, Fibonacci, goes missing during their first slumber party of the summer. The girls must use their combined STEAM skills in order to find and rescue Fibbo. But they quickly discover that their search and rescue mission is just the beginning of their epic adventure.

While this Lessons Plan book is structured to enable kids to perform STEM/STEAM activities related to each chapter of the STEAMTEAM 5 book, owning the book is not required.

To learn more about our mission and our book series, please visit www.STEAMTEAM5.com.

We hope you enjoy these activities as much as we do!

Lesson 1: Identifying Aquatic Insects

Description: This lesson is designed to help children use their skills to make and record scientific observations about aquatic insects.

Duration: 45 Minutes

Content	Assessed in this Lesson?
Science	Yes
Technology	
Engineering	
Art	
Mathematics	

Learning Objectives & Outcomes:

Your student(s) will be able to identify the type of insects found in different forms of moving water.

Materials Required:

- Water with aquatic insects from two different locations (be sure to label the water)
- Biotic Index Cards of Aquatic Insects (see Educator Resources)
- One red marker
- One blue marker
- Two large plastic containers or glass jars for water
- A magnifying glass
- A notebook

Teacher Instruction:

1. Explain the different types of natural running water found near you, such as:

    - Stream
    - Creek
    - River
    - Swamp
    - Bayou
    - Brook
    - Seaway

2. Choose two different water sources that you will be observing. Explain to your student(s) that they will be observing both types and comparing the insects that live in both.

3. Collect water samples in either clear plastic containers or large glass jars. If it's safe to do so, include your student(s) in this step. Label each water sample and be sure to keep the two types of water samples separate.

Educator Resources:

- http://www.differencebetween.com/difference-between-stream-and-vs-river/
- http://pediaa.com/difference-between-creek-and-stream/
- https://en.wikipedia.org/wiki/Body_of_water#Waterbody_types
- https://en.wikipedia.org/wiki/Biotic_index
- http://ecosystems.psu.edu/youth/sftrc/lesson-plan-pdfs/BioticIndexCard.pdf
- http://participatoryscience.org/sites/default/files/riverkey.jpg

Procedure

1. Set up a workstation with the following supplies:

   - A key to the aquatic insects (Example: Biotic Index Cards of Aquatic Insects),

   - A red marker,

   - A blue marker,

   - A notebook, and

   - A magnifying glass.

2. Ensuring that you've labeled each of the two water samples, place them at the workstation.

3. Have the student draw a chart like the following in his/her notebook.

Water Sample #1	Water Sample #2

4. Using the magnifying glass, find an insect in the first water container (i.e., Water Sample #1).

5. Use the key to identify the insect in the first water sample.

6. Draw a red circle around the image of the insect on the key, then write the name of the insect under the Water Sample #1 heading in the notebook.

7. Continue to identify insects and record your findings under Water Sample #1 in the notebook for 10-15 more minutes.

8. Find an insect in the second water container.

9. Use the key to identify the insect in the second water sample.

10. Draw a blue circle around the image of the insect in the second water sample on the key, then write the name of the insect under the Water Sample #2 heading in the notebook.

11. Continue to identify insects and record your findings under Water Sample #2 in the notebook for 10-15 more minutes.

12. Review the insects found in each water sample and observe the similarities and differences between the two. Note these observations in the notebook.

Assessment & Evaluation:

- What conclusions can be made about the water and the insects from each water source?
- Review the student's notes in his/her notepad to assess their understanding of the material.

Lesson 2: Creating an Algorithm

Description: This lesson is designed to teach children the concept of an algorithm and how to create a basic algorithm of their own.

Duration: 60 Minutes

Content	Assessed in this Lesson?
Science	
Technology	Yes
Engineering	
Art	
Mathematics	Yes

Learning Objectives & Outcomes:

Your student will be able to explain what an algorithm is and will be able to create a simple one of their own.

Materials Required:

- pencil
- STEAMTEAM 5 algorithm grid

Teacher Instruction:

1. Ask your student(s) to imagine that they're explaining to someone how to brush their teeth. Have them explain using step-by-step instructions (e.g. Step 1: Wet the toothbrush. Step 2: Squeeze a pea-sized amount of toothpaste onto the toothbrush. Step 3: Brush the upper left side of your teeth, etc.)

   - Note: If they skip a step, make sure to remind them to include every step in the right order.

2. Ask your student(s) the following questions:
   - What could happen if you gave all of the instructions at once?
   - What could happen if you gave the instructions in the wrong order?
   - Why is it important for you to give instructions in the correct order?

3. Explain to your student(s) that many of the tasks we complete in our daily lives involve a series of steps which must be followed in a particular order.

Procedure

1. Using the STEAMTEAM 5 algorithm grid on the following page, explain to your student(s) that they will need to create step-by-step instructions to guide Treeka (in the first row of the first column) to her drone by advancing only one square at a time.

    > This is Treeka. She lost her drone. Your job is to direct Treeka the drone by guiding her one square at a time. Decide which direction Treeka will travel in each step. When you are happy with your directions, draw arrows on the grid to demonstrate the path she will take.

2. Ask your student(s) to draw one arrow at a time showing the pathway from Treeka to the drone. Explain that there is more than one pathway Treeka could take to reach the drone.

3. Once the pathway is drawn using a series of arrows, have your student(s) write a set of directions on a blank piece of paper next to the grid that explains the steps Treeka must take using directional language. (For example, Step 1: Move Treeka to right one square. Step 2: Move Treeka down one square, and so on.)

4. Explain to your student(s) that lists of instructions such as these are called "algorithms."

Assessment & Evaluation:

*   Ask your student(s) to explain what an algorithm is.
*   Test your student(s) algorithm to ensure that all of the steps are provided to guide Treeka to her controller.
*   Ask your student(s) how they could make the algorithm harder.

STEAMTEAM™ 5 Algorithm Grid

Lesson 3: Building a Bridge STEM Challenge

Description: This lesson is designed to help children gain an understanding of materials used in the construction of bridges.

Duration: 2 hours

Content	Assessed in this Lesson?
Science	Yes
Technology	Yes
Engineering	Yes
Art	Yes
Mathematics	Yes

Learning Objectives & Outcomes:

- Your student(s) will be able to describe four different types of bridges (beam, arch, suspension, and cantilever);
- Your student(s) will be able to plan, design, build, and test a bridge made from everyday household materials.

Materials Required:

- At least 5 toy cars (such as Hotwheels™ or Matchbox™)
- Brainstorm some common classroom materials that might be suitable for building your bridge (these need to be readily available in your classroom). Once you have decided upon the materials that are available for use, list these items below.

Teacher Instruction:

1. Read this scenario to your student(s):

   Recently, the bridge that spans the river in a nearby town was demolished. It was extremely old and was no longer safe for cars. The town must now build a new bridge to span the river, and they need your help.

   The Challenge: Design and build a bridge that spans a gap of 20 inches (between two tables) and supports the weight of a moving toy car.

2. Read these rules to your student(s):
   - The bridge must be free standing. It cannot be attached to the tables.

- The bridge may only be constructed using the materials from the agreed list.
- The bridge must be completed within 2 hours.

Educator Resources:

- http://www.historyofbridges.com/facts-about-bridges/types-of-bridges/
- https://en.wikipedia.org/wiki/List_of_bridge_types

Procedure

1. Explain these different types of bridges: beam, arch, suspension, and cantilever. Look at some images of each type of bridge online.

2. Have your student(s) complete the **Types of Bridges** worksheet provided in this lesson by drawing an example of each type of bridge and listing the features, building materials used, and one famous example for each bridge type.

3. Have your student(s) list the materials that they are going to use for each part of your bridge. Have them explain why they have chosen each material. (For example, I chose cardboard for the road because it is sturdy enough to support a toy car.)

4. Have your student(s) draw a detailed diagram of your bridge. Label each part.

5. Have your student(s) build the bridge. (Take a photo!)

6. Once the bridge is built, it is time to test it! Your student's goal is for their bridge to support the weight of a moving toy car. As a bonus challenge, see how many toy cars their bridge can support at once.

7. Discuss the success of your student's bridge design by answering the following questions.

   a. Did your bridge achieve the goal of the task? Explain why you feel your bridge design was or was not successful.

   b. What affected the decisions you made when selecting materials for the bridge?

      Engineers must also make decisions about which materials to use when constructing bridges. For example, they often consider the sustainability of materials, which means that they consider whether the material is harmful to the environment or whether it depletes natural resources. Some factors that affect the sustainability of a material include what it is made from, how it's produced, how available it is, and whether it can be recycled or reused. Discuss the sustainability of these materials: wood, steel, and plastic.

Assessment & Evaluation:

- Did your student's bridge support the weight of a moving toy car?
- Was their bridge able to support additional toy cars?
- How many toy cars was their bridge able to support?

Type of Bridges

Beam Bridge	Features:
	Building Materials:
	Famous Example:

Arch Bridge	Features:
	Building Materials:
	Famous Example:

Suspension Bridge	Features:
	Building Materials:
	Famous Example:

Cantilever Bridge	Features:
	Building Materials:
	Famous Example:

Lesson 4: Principles of Design - Symmetry

Description: This lesson is designed to teach your student(s) about the principle of art called "balance" and how it can be used in an artwork.

Duration: 30-45 Minutes

Content	Assessed in this Lesson?
Science	Yes
Technology	
Engineering	
Art	Yes
Mathematics	

Learning Objectives & Outcomes:

- Your student(s) will be able to explain the principle of art called "balance."
- Your student(s) will be able to explain the concept of "symmetry."
- Your student(s) will be able to identify symmetry in nature.

Materials Required:

- A mirror
- Construction paper
- Scissors
- Watercolors or tempera paints
- Geometric shapes (tangrams)
- A photo of a person

Teacher Instruction:

1. Explain that symmetry means having exactly the same thing on both sides. In other words, it's a mirror image.
2. Explain that symmetry adds balance to a design and can be found in nature.
3. Show your student(s) pictures of different things that have symmetry, then pictures of things in nature that have symmetry. Ask your student(s) the question: "What do you notice about these things?" (Your student(s) should answer that they look the same on both sides.)
4. Draw a line down the photo of the person. Describe the symmetry of the human body (two eyes, two ears, two arms and two legs).
5. Demonstrate how the geometric shapes will turn into a full symmetrical object when you hold them against a mirror.

Procedure

1. Have your student(s) draw some shapes on the construction paper then cut them out.
2. Ask your student(s) to fold the shapes in such a way to demonstrate symmetry.
3. Have your student(s) hold the (unfolded) geometric shapes perpendicular against a mirror; ask them to explain what they see.
4. Have your student(s) create an original painting that incorporates symmetrical balance.

Assessment & Evaluation:

- Your students are able to identify symmetry in nature.
- The students' painting incorporates symmetrical balance, demonstrating an understanding of that principle of design.

Lesson 5: Slumber Party Planning

Description: This lesson is designed to teach your student(s) how to calculate area as well as the concept of "form follows function."

Duration: 30-45 Minutes

Content	Assessed in this Lesson?
Science	
Technology	
Engineering	
Art	Yes
Mathematics	Yes

Learning Objectives & Outcomes:

- Your student(s) will be able to explain the how to calculate area.
- Your student(s) will be able to explain the concept of "form follows function."

Materials Required:

- The Tent Floor Plan and Gear pages
- Scissors
- Pencil

Teacher Instruction:

1. Explain how to calculate the area of something. (Area is measured in square units such as square inches, square feet or square meters. To find the area of a rectangle, you would multiply the length by the width.)
2. Explain that you measure things such as a bedroom in your house by calculating the area of the room. Give an example such as this: If your bedroom is 10 feet wide by 10 feet long, you have a 100 square foot bedroom.
3. Explain that just because your bedroom is 100 square feet in area, that doesn't mean you have 100 square feet worth of room for toys, clothes, a bed, and other personal items. After all, you need room to walk, play with your toys, and so on.

Procedure

1. Print and distribute the Tent Floor Plan and Gear on the following pages. (Copy those pages for multiple students)
2. Pose the following scenario to your student(s):

   You are hosting a slumber party in your backyard for your friends. Your tent is 14 feet long and 9 feet wide. How many sleeping bags can you fit into it for your slumber party?

3. Explain that each square on the Tent Floor Plan represents one square foot.
4. Explain how to calculate 14 x 9 to get 126.
5. Ask your student(s) to estimate how many sleeping bags will fit inside the tent (before they place any sleeping bags into the floor plan).
6. Have the student(s) measure one sleeping bag using the Tent Floor Plan. How big is the sleeping bag? (It should be 2 feet wide by 5 feet long, which is 10 square feet.)
7. Have the student(s) arrange the sleeping bags onto the Tent Floor Plan, fitting in as many sleeping bags as they can without overlapping them (or having them cross the outer boundary of the tent).
8. Leaving the sleeping bags in place on the Tent Floor Plan, ask your student(s) how many sleeping bags they were able to fit in their tent.
9. Now, ask your student(s) to consider the following: How will the tent occupants be able to move around inside of the tent without stepping on each other? Where will the lanterns go?
10. Instruct your student(s) to make changes to their Tent Floor Plan to accommodate the two lanterns and foot traffic (i.e., walking inside of the tent). Have them draw a path where the occupants are able to move around in the tent.
11. Observe how many sleeping bags will now fit in the Tent Floor Plan.
12. Ask your students to explain why it's important to know how an area (such as a tent) is going to be used when you are planning an event.

Assessment & Evaluation:

- Your student(s) are able to measure area.
- Your student(s) will be able to explain why it's important to know how something will be used when you are creating it.

Tent Floor Plan

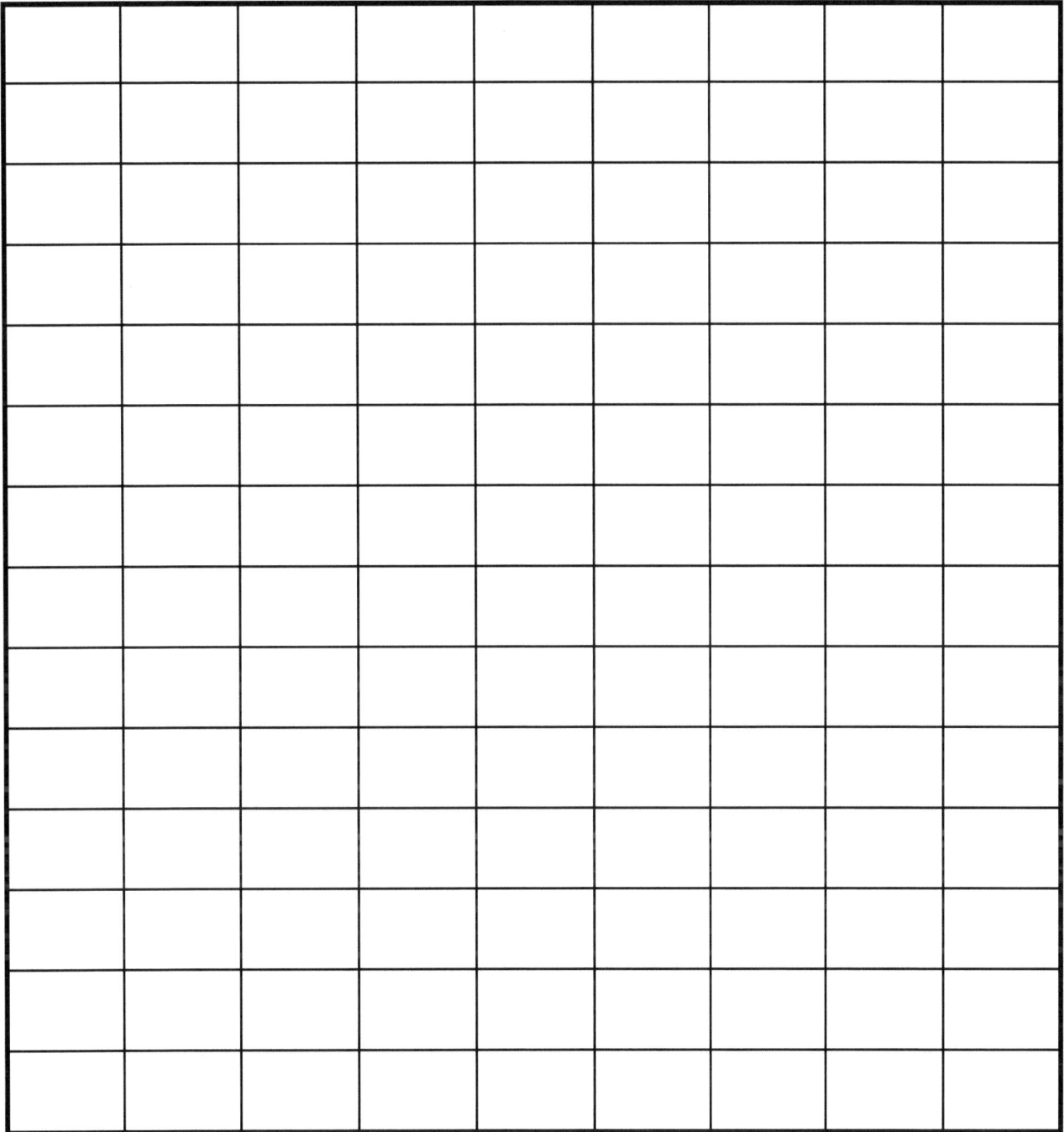

Gear

Sleeping Bags

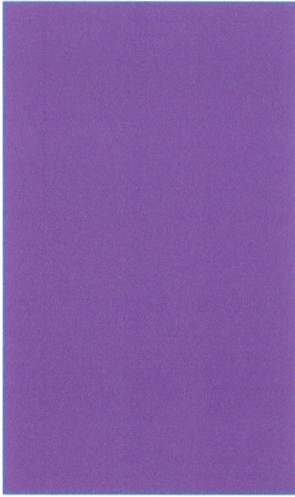 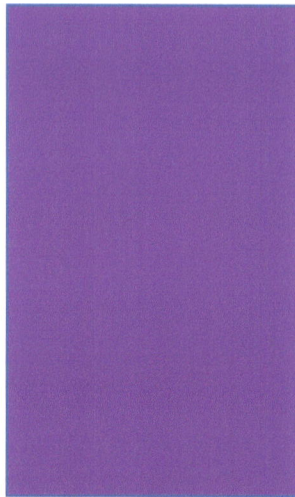 

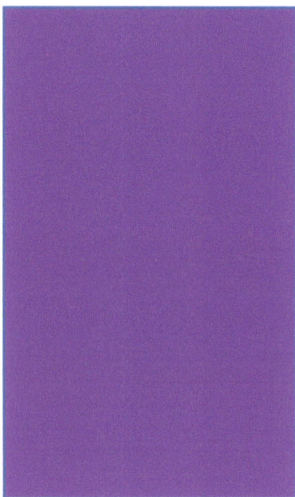  

Lanterns

Bonus Lesson 5: Estimating

Description: This lesson is designed to teach your student(s) how to perform a simple statistical analysis of the frequency of colors of M&Ms in a bag.

Duration: 90 Minutes

Content	Assessed in this Lesson?
Science	
Technology	
Engineering	
Art	
Mathematics	Yes

Learning Objectives & Outcomes:

- Your student(s) will learn what a statistical average is and how to calculate it.
- Your student(s) will learn about recording experimental data.
- Your student(s) will learn how to create and label a bar chart and a pie chart.
- Your student(s) will learn how an average can help predict the distribution of a given sample (i.e., predict the number of each color candy within an M&Ms bag).

Materials Required:

- 5 bags (standard 1.69-ounce size) of M&Ms (or Skittles or other candy that comes in multiple colors)
- 1 king size bag of M&Ms
- The Candy Data Table provided in this lesson
    - **Note:** We also included a completed Candy Data Table as an example.
- Polar graph paper (or Excel)
- Colored pencils, markers, or crayons for the bar chart, if needed.

Teacher Instruction:

1. Ask your student(s) this question: Can you predict how often you will pick a green M&M if you reach your hand into this bag? (Hold up a large bag of M&Ms.)

2. Explain statistics as follows:

Statistics are facts or data based on a set of **numerical information**. The set of information is often about a certain group, such as a group of people. The statistics are used as a numerical way to describe that group.

Here's an example:

Think about kids on a playground. This group of kids would be called the **population** in statistics terms. Some numerical information that you could collect about the playground would be the number of boys and girls you see there, the height of each child, the age of each child, and so on. You could then take this numerical information and use it to draw certain conclusions about the playground, such as the percentage of kids who are female and the average age of a child on that playground. These facts are *statistics* about that playground.

Sometimes statistics can be unpredictable, which means that they don't have any type of pattern. In other words, the numerical information they are based on appears to be *random*. However, many statistics do have patterns and those patterns can be used to make **models**, form **hypotheses**, and make **predictions** about specific things. For example, if you figured out the average age of the kids on the playground, that statistic could help you predict the age of kids at a similar playground in a different neighborhood.

4. Pose the following question to your student(s): What would you do if you wanted to know how many kids on the playground are 5 years old?

5. Explain the following approach to answering that question:

   You could ask every child his/her age, count how many kids are five years old, and then compare that number to the total number of kids on the playground.

   In statistics, how often a certain **event** happens, such as a student being five years old, is referred to as the **frequency** of that event. In the example I shared, frequency can be measured by counting the numbers of each of the different ages of the kids on the playground.

6. Explain the goal of this lesson:

   In this lesson, we will determine the frequency of different colored M&Ms in a bag of M&M candies. There are six different colors: blue, red, orange, green, yellow, and brown.

Educator Resources:

- https://nces.ed.gov/nceskids/CreateAGraph/default.aspx (for bar graph)
- http://www.purplemath.com/modules/percntof.htm (explaining percentages)

Procedure

1. Print out the **Candy Data Table** on page 27. You'll use this to track your data.

2. Open the first small bag of M&Ms. Count the number of M&Ms of each color and write the numbers in your data table (see our example). Do not eat any of the M&Ms before you count them!

3. Repeat step 2 for each remaining small bags of M&Ms.

   Note: You should sample at least five bags. Remember: The more samples you take, the more accurate your data will be.

4. Calculate the **total number of M&Ms in each bag** by adding each column. For each bag, write the answer in the "Whole Bag" box in the bottom row of your data table.

5. Calculate the **total number of each color in all of the bags combined** by adding across each row. Then, calculate the total number of M&Ms in all of the bags combined. Write the answers in the "Total" column of your data table.

6. Calculate the **average number of each candy color per bag**. Do this by dividing the total numbers you calculated in step 5 by the number of packages (which should be 5 or more). Write the answers in the "Average" column for each color in your data table.

7. Calculate the **average number of candies per bag**. Write the answer in the "Average" column on the "Whole Bag" row in your data table. (This is 57.2 in the example we provided.)

8. Explain to your student(s) what a percentage is and how to calculate it. Then, calculate the percentage of each colored M&M per bag using the average data. Do this calculation by dividing the average number of each color (calculated in step 6) by the average number of M&Ms in the whole bag and then multiplying your answer by 100. Write your answers in the "Percentage" column in your data table.

   In our example, there are an average of 10.4 green M&Ms in each bag and an average of 57.2 M&Ms in a whole bag, so we divided 10.4 by 57.2 (which equals 0.1818) and then multiplied it by 100 (which gave us 18.18%). **Note:** If you do this same calculation with your whole bag data, you should get 100%. Also, round up to the nearest whole number if you want to make this easier.

11. Explain to your student(s) that statistics allows us to predict the percentage of M&Ms by color in a larger bag of M&Ms. We would expect the smaller and larger packets to have about the same percentage of each color.

12. Make a bar chart using the data from the "Average" column of your data table. In our example, it would look like this.

Average

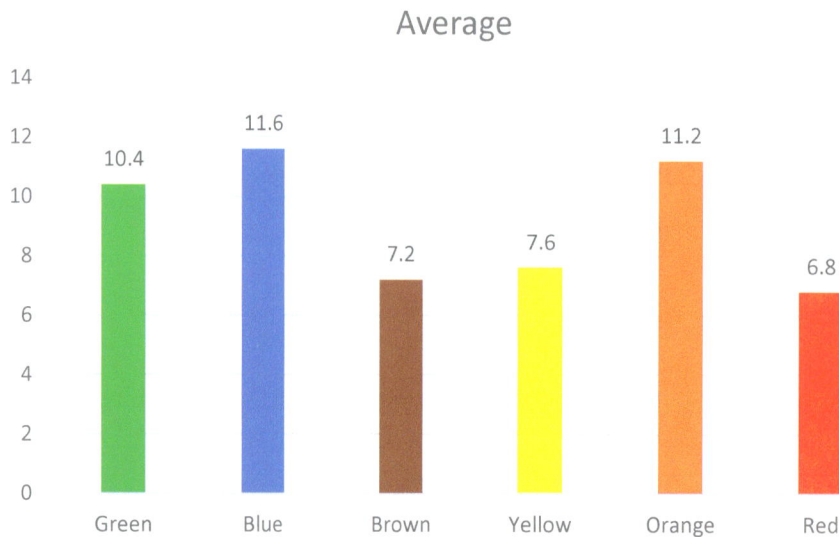

13. This bar chart shows the average frequency of each color of M&M in a bag. It's useful for comparing the frequencies of each individual color to each of the other individual colors.

How to create a bar chart:

Label the y-axis (the vertical axis going up and down) with a scale representing the average numbers of M&Ms. The smallest number of the scale will be zero and the largest number of the scale (maximum) should be set just above the largest average number of M&Ms in any color. (See the example above.)

On the x-axis of the bar graph (the horizontal axis going left and right), make a bar for each color. Make the bar go up to the number on the y-axis that corresponds to the average number of M&Ms counted for that color. Label each bar with the correct color (and, if possible, color in the bar with the matching color too).

14. Looking at your data in the bar chart, ask your student(s) to answer these questions:

   - In the average bag of M&Ms, which color are most of the M&Ms (highest frequency)?

   - Which color is the rarest (lowest frequency)?

- Do any of the colors have the same frequencies?

- Do you see any other trends in your data in the bar chart?

15. Now you are ready to make your second graph, the pie chart, using the data from the "Percentage" column of your data table. It will tell you which portion of the whole bag is of each color. It is useful for comparing the **relative proportion** of each individual color to the whole population of M&Ms.

    Using Excel or polar graph paper, make a pie chart where each slice is equal to the percentage of one of the colors. Label each slice with the color it represents. Here's an example of a pie chart we made in Excel using the data from our example:

Percentage

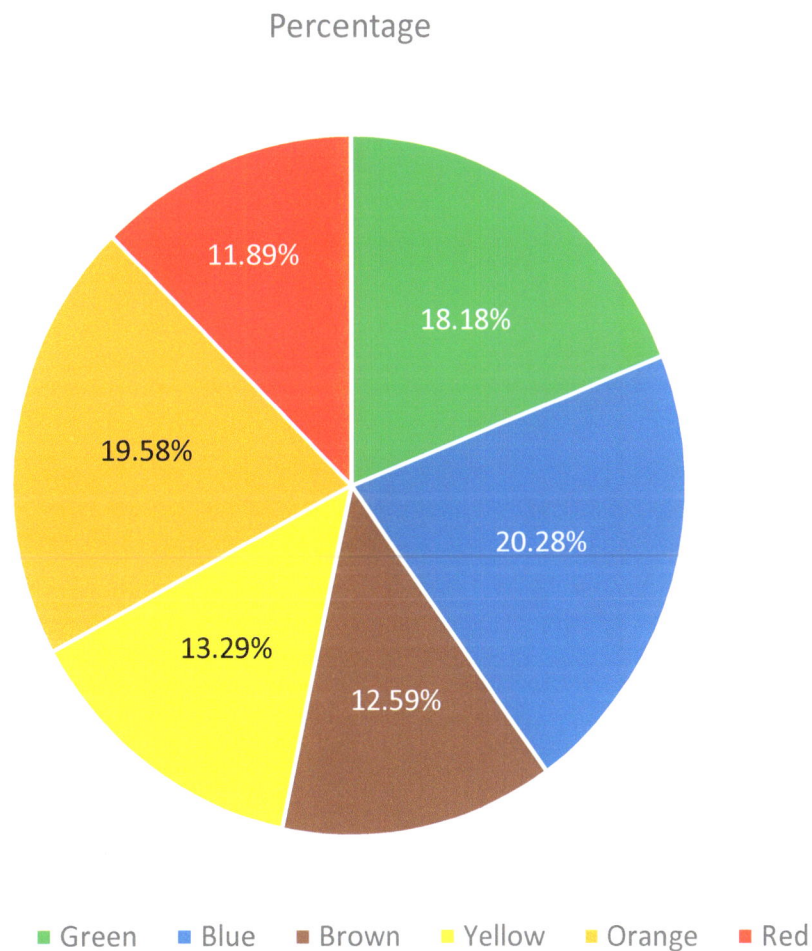

■ Green ■ Blue ■ Brown ■ Yellow ■ Orange ■ Red

16. Looking at your data in the pie chart, try to answer the following questions:

- What is the percentage of each color of M&M in the package?

- Does any color make up more than half of a package? What about more than a third of the package?

17. Looking at your data table and graphs, do you think you can predict what color(s) M&M you are most likely to pick from a bag? If so, what color(s) is it?

Assessment & Evaluation:

- Your student(s) can explain what a statistical average is and how to calculate it.
- Your student(s) created a bar chart that accurately reflected averages.
- Your student(s) created a pie chart that accurately reflected percentages.

Candy Data Table (example)

| Color | Small Package of M&Ms | | | | | Total | Average | Percentage |
	Bag 1	Bag 2	Bag 3	Bag 4	Bag 5			
Green	10	11	10	10	11	52	10.4	18.18%
Blue	14	13	14	13	14	58	11.6	20.28%
Brown	8	7	7	7	7	36	7.2	12.59%
Yellow	8	7	8	7	8	38	7.6	13.29%
Orange	12	11	11	11	11	56	11.2	19.58%
Red	7	8	7	7	7	34	6.8	11.89%
Whole bag	59	57	57	55	58	286	57.2	

Candy Data Table (to be completed)

| Color | Small Package of M&Ms | | | | | Total | Average | Percentage |
	Bag 1	Bag 2	Bag 3	Bag 4	Bag 5			
Green								
Blue								
Brown								
Yellow								
Orange								
Red								
Whole bag								

Lesson 6: Encryption: Making a Cipher Wheel

Description: This lesson is designed to help children learn how simple encryption works.

Duration: 60 Minutes

Content	Assessed in this Lesson?
Science	
Technology	Yes
Engineering	
Art	
Mathematics	

Learning Objectives & Outcomes:

- Your student(s) will be able to explain how basic encryption works.
- Your student(s) will be able to create a cipher wheel and use it to encrypt and decrypt a message.

Materials Required:

- Cipher wheel template (one is provided in this document)
- One Round brad fastener/split pin
- One piece of paper
- A pencil

Teacher Instruction:

- Explain what a cipher wheel is: A cipher wheel is a wheel that has the alphabet printed on it. There's a second, smaller wheel mounted in the center of it that also has the same alphabet printed on it. The inner wheel can be rotated so that any letter on one wheel can be aligned with any letter on the outer wheel.

- Explain how cipher wheels have been used for secret correspondence throughout history. Here are some examples:

    a. The Roman ruler Julius Caesar (100 B.C. – 44 B.C.) used a very simple cipher for secret communication. He substituted each letter of the alphabet with a letter that was three positions further along in the alphabet. (So, an "A" would be replaced with a "D.") Later, any cipher that used this "displacement" concept was referred to as a Caesar cipher.

b. Thomas Jefferson used a cipher wheel to encode and decode messages during the American Revolution.

c. The Confederate Cipher Disc was a mechanical wheel consisting of two discs, each with the 26 letters of the Latin alphabet. It was used for encrypting secret messages of the Confederacy during the American Civil War (1861-1865)

Educator Resources:

- https://www.monticello.org/site/research-and-collections/wheel-cipher
- http://www.cs.trincoll.edu/~crypto/historical/alberti.html
- http://ciphermachines.com/jefferson
- https://en.wikipedia.org/wiki/Cipher_disk
- http://www.civilwarsignals.org/pages/crypto/cipherdisk.html
- http://www.cryptomuseum.com/crypto/usa/ccd/index.htm

Procedure

1. Print the cipher wheels provided on the following pages. Cut the wheels out. (You can glue them onto heavy stock paper or paper plates if you want them to last longer.)

2. Write the alphabet in the outer boxes of both the small and large wheel.

3. Use a sharp pencil to punch a hole though the center of both wheels. Push the paper fastener (split pin/brad fastener) through the small wheel and then through the larger wheel, then open the split pin at the back so that the wheels are fastened together.

4. Line up the letter As on both wheels. Make sure they are pointing upward.

5. Choose two letters (one from each wheel) that will be your secret letters. You will need to remember these letters and share them with the person who will be decoding your message.

6. Line your two chosen letters up so they are both pointing upward. You'll notice that the other letters no longer match around the wheels.

7. Ask your student(s) to compose a secret note by looking for the letter you want to use on the smaller wheel and replacing it with the letter above it on the larger wheel.

8. Use the cipher wheel your student(s) created to compose a secret message, then have your student(s) decrypt it.

Assessment & Evaluation:

1. Your student(s) can explain what encryption means.

2. Your student(s) can create a cipher wheel and used it to encrypt and decrypt a message.

Large Wheel

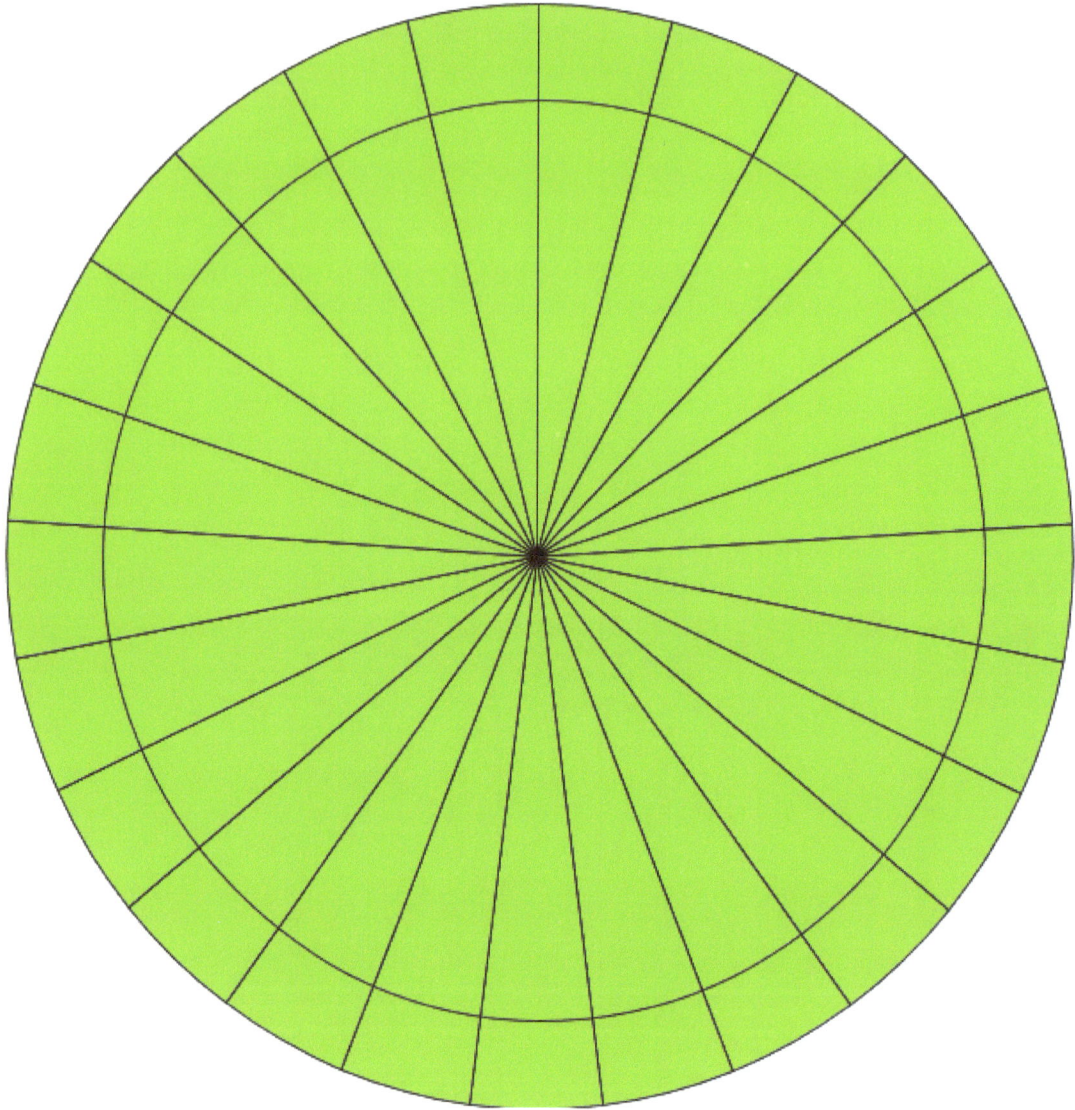

Small Wheel

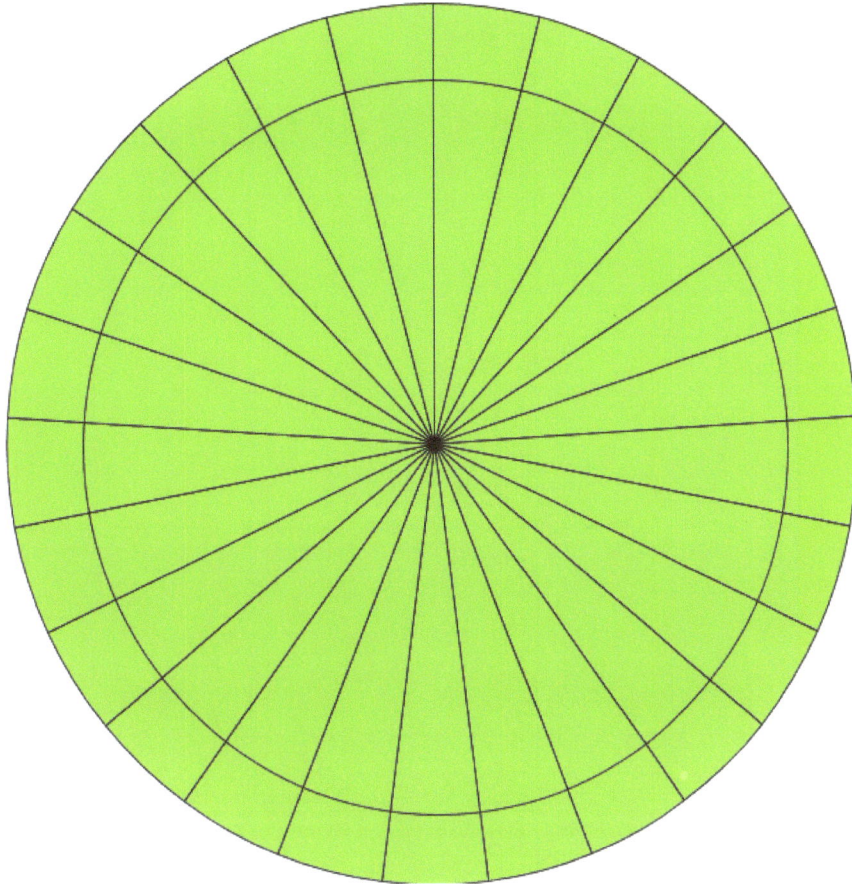

Lesson 7: Identifying Animal Tracks

Description: This lesson is designed to teach children how to set up a tracking station in order to learn what types of animals live nearby.

Duration: 2 hours (over 2 days)

Content	Assessed in this Lesson?
Science	Yes
Technology	
Engineering	
Art	
Mathematics	

Learning Objectives & Outcomes:

- Your student(s) will be able to set up a tracking station.
- Your student(s) will learn how to use a field guide to identify common animal tracks.

Materials Required:

- One piece of plywood (at least 2x2 feet)
- A small dog/cat dish, a block of wood, or a shallow bowl that is on the heavy side (hard to drag away)
- Peanut butter
- Cereal
- Mud (dirt mixed with water)
- An animal tracks field guide
- Science journal/notebook

Teacher Instruction:

- Explain to your student(s) that there are ways to learn about what types of animals live near you without ever seeing one. One way is to set up a tracking station to record the presence and/or activity of animals.

Educator Resources:

- https://www.amazon.com/s/ref=nb_sb_noss?url=search-alias%3Dstripbooks&field-keywords=Guide+to+Animal+Tracks
- https://www.google.com/search?q=animal+tracks+field+guide
- https://www.fws.gov/uploadedFiles/Animal%20Signs%20Guide.pdf
- https://itunes.apple.com/us/app/itrack-wildlife/id478516226?mt=8

Procedure

1. Mix the mud in a large bucket or container. Aim for the consistency of peanut butter, but make it thinner if you live in a dry area to keep the water from evaporating before the animals come to the station.

2. Before the sun goes down, spread the mud smoothly over the plywood.

3. Spread some peanut butter onto the dish/block of wood/bowl, then sprinkle some cereal on it. (Make sure you use enough peanut butter to make the cereal stick.)

4. Place the bait "dish" in the center of the mud-covered plywood. This is your tracking station.

5. Place the tracking station on a flat (level) surface in the backyard.

   Notes:

   - Animals are more likely to hang out and make footprints if they feel safe, so don't place your tracking station in a vulnerable area such as out in the open.
   - If your yard backs up to the woods or a field, place the tracking station there.
   - If you don't back up to the woods or a field, place the tracking station outside of a fenced back yard or near bushes or trees.

6. The next morning, grab your field guide and head to the tracking station as early as possible after the sun rises. Check the tracking station for tracks. If you see any tracks, refer to your field guide to note the types of tracks you've found in your science journal.

7. "Re-set" the tracking station by smoothing out the mud and replacing the food. Sometimes different animals come to it on different nights or different types of food attract different animals.

8. The next morning, check the tracking station to see if any different animals left tracks. Note all of the tracks you identified in your science journal.

Assessment & Evaluation:

- Your student(s) can tell you which types of animals live near them.

Lesson 8: Creating a Heat Detector

Description: This lesson is designed to teach children how heat detection works and how to create a heat detector.

Duration: 20 Minutes

Content	Assessed in this Lesson?
Science	Yes
Technology	Yes
Engineering	Yes
Art	
Mathematics	

Learning Objectives & Outcomes:

- Your student(s) will be able to demonstrate how heat detection works.
- Your student(s) will be able to demonstrate heat detection.

Materials Required:

- One thin nail
- One rubber band
- Cardboard (the size of the wooden block)
- Scissors
- A wooden block that is large enough for the rubber band to stretch around the edge of it
- Some matches, a lighter, or a candle

Teacher Instruction:

- The goal of this project is to demonstrate the expansion and contraction of materials when heat is applied to them. In this case, the material you are trying to heat is the rubber band.

- You only need one source of heat: a match, a lighter, or a candle. Of course, we recommend that you, the instructor, operate the heat source.

Procedure

1. Create the heat gauge as follows:

    a. Cut an arrow shape out of the cardboard. The length of the arrow should be the same as the wooden block.

    b. Wrap the rubber band around the wooden block.

    c. Insert the thin nail through the central base of the arrow cardboard.

    d. Position the thin nail in the center of one side of the block, between the block and the rubber band.

        Note: Your gauge should look like this:

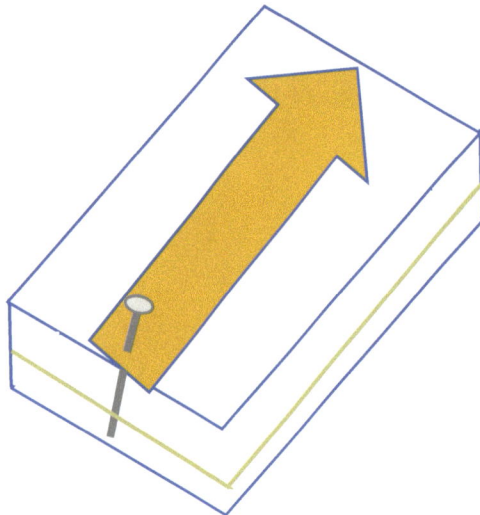

2. Test the heat gauge as follows:

    a. Light the heat source (match, lighter, or candle) and place it next to the rubber band near the nail. Your arrow should begin turning in a counterclockwise direction now.

    b. Move the heat source to the opposite side and notice how the arrow moves.

Discuss the Following Observation:

Notice that as soon as we applied heat on the rubber material, the rubber band started to contract, causing the nail to rotate, which moved the arrow. After we moved the source of heat to the other side, the heated portion of the rubber band was changed, and the previous side cooled down.

You should have noticed that the arrow started moving in the opposite direction after we changed the placement of the heat.

Here's what really happened: The rubber band contracted when heat was applied to it, and then it expanded as soon as the same area cooled down. This is the reason the arrow moved.

Assessment & Evaluation:

- Your student(s) can explain why the arrow moved when heat was next to the rubber band.

Lesson 9: Simple Machines - Making a Lever

Description: This lesson is designed to teach children about simple machines. They'll create one common type of simple machine that they have likely encountered on a playground: a lever.

Duration: 30 Minutes

Content	Assessed in this Lesson?
Science	
Technology	
Engineering	Yes
Art	
Mathematics	

Learning Objectives & Outcomes:

- Your student(s) will be able to explain what a simple machine is.
- Your student(s) will be able to explain how a lever works and the role the fulcrum plays.
- Your student(s) will be able to share examples of a lever.

Materials Required:

- A wooden ruler
- A large binder clip
- Tape
- 10 pennies

Teacher Instruction:

- Explain what a simple machine is:

  Machines make work easier by creating a force that is a push or pull that make an object move. A simple machine makes work easier by changing the direction of a force, the size of the force or both. One example of a simple machine is a lever.

  A lever is strong bar that is used to lift and move something heavy. The bar rests on a fulcrum; when you apply force on one end of the bar, you can move an object on the other end.

- Today we are going to prove that a lever makes work easier.

Procedure

1. Remove the metal clips from the base of the binder clip by squeezing the sides together and slipping the ends out of the groove. The binder clip will become the fulcrum, which is the part that gives your lever a pivot point.

2. Place the ruler on top of the binder clip. Position the binder clip (fulcrum) near the middle so that the two ends of the ruler are perfectly balanced. (Hint: The balance point should be at about the 15 cm (6 inch) mark on the ruler.)

3. Place a stack of 5 pennies on each end of the ruler: one stack on the 1 cm (1 in.) side and the other 5 pennies on the very edge of the 30 cm (12 inch) side. The two stacks of pennies weigh the same, so the two ends of the ruler should remain balanced.

4. Remove 3 of the pennies from one end of the ruler and add them to the stack on the other end. (One end should have 2 pennies and one end should have 8 pennies.) Notice what happens to the ends of the ruler. (The ruler should be tilted down on the side with the 8 pennies.)

5. Move the fulcrum (binder clip) toward the end with the 8 pennies on it until that end is raised up. You have just made a lever and used it to lift a heavy object with a lighter one!

6. Observe what happens when you move the fulcrum back and forth while changing the placement of the pennies.

Discuss the Following Observation:

In this experiment, you took a basic ruler and added a fulcrum to make a simple machine called a lever!

One very common example of a lever is a seesaw. If you have a heavier person on one end, the lighter person on the other end of the lever will raise up.

In our experiment, by moving the fulcrum closer to the heavy end, you were able to use the lever to help you raise the heavier stack using a lighter one on the opposite end. This didn't change anything about the lighter weight—it stayed exactly the same.

Moving the fulcrum (the pivot point) closer to the larger stack of pennies we were trying to lift changed how much force (or work) it took to lift those 8 pennies. It made it much easier to lift a larger stack of pennies.

What happens when you moved the fulcrum away from the larger stack of pennies? Answer: It takes more force, or in this example, a heavier weight to lift the object!

Assessment & Evaluation:

- Your student(s) can explain what a simple machine does.
- Your student(s) can explain how a lever works.

Lesson 10: Patterns in Nature

Description: This lesson is designed to teach children about the Fibonacci (pronounced fib-o-nawch-ee) sequence and how to use it to create a Golden Rectangle.

Duration: 60 Minutes

Content	Assessed in this Lesson?
Science	Yes
Technology	
Engineering	
Art	Yes
Mathematics	Yes

Learning Objectives & Outcomes:

- Your student(s) will be able to explain Fibonacci numbers.
- Your student(s) will be able to identify Fibonacci numbers in nature and art.
- Your student(s) will be able to write the Fibonacci sequence.
- Your student(s) will be able to create the Golden Rectangle.

Materials Required:

- A piece of paper
- A ruler
- Graph paper
- A compass
- Colored pencils

Teacher Instruction:

- Explain what the Fibonacci sequence is:

    In mathematics, the Fibonacci sequence is a series of numbers in which each number equals the sum of the two numbers before it. It always starts with the numbers "0" and "1."

The sequence shown below is 0, 1, 1, 2, 3, 5, 8, 13, and 21.

So, after the first "0" and "1," the math looks like this:

- o 0+1=1
- o 1+1=2
- o 1+2=3
- o 2+3=5
- o 3+5=8
- o 5+8=13
- o 8+13=21

- Show your student(s) some examples of the Fibonacci sequence found in nature, and show them the illustration below as an example:

This Nautilus seashell is an example of Fibonacci's sequence, which is sometimes called the *Golden Spiral*. Notice that the spirals on this shell expand with every quarter, or 90 degree, turn from the center.

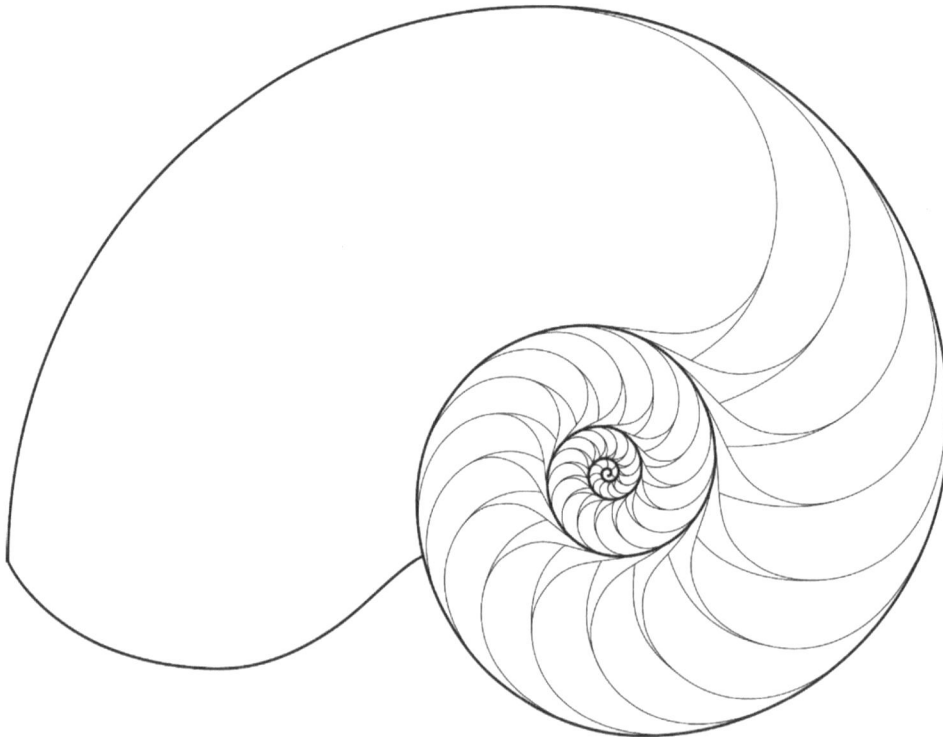

Procedure

1. Complete the following Fibonacci sequence:

   0, 1, 1, 2, 3, 5, __ , __ , __ , __ ,

2. Using your graph paper, start by coloring in a 1x1 square. Then, color in another 1x1 square right next to it using a different colored pencil. Here's an example:

3. Next, add a 2x2 square below it like this:

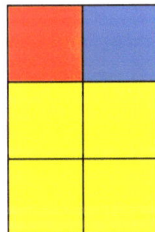

4. Next, add a 3x3 square to the right like this:

5. Next, add a 5x5 square. Where do you think it should go?

6. Look at Step #1 again. What size square should you add next?

7. Share this observation with your student(s): The interesting thing about making rectangles like this is that the ratio (the number that shows how the sides relate to each other) always stays the same, no matter how big the rectangle gets. This ratio is called the Golden Ratio. The rectangles it creates are called "Golden Rectangles" because they are said to be the most beautiful rectangles to look at. You can find the ratio by dividing the long side by the short side. For example, if you have a rectangle that is 3 × 5, you would divide 5 by 3. This will give us a number that is about 1.61.

8. Next, we'll create a Golden Rectangle on the large sheet of paper. Start by drawing two squares side by side again. (Use your ruler to make them 0.5 cm wide.)

9. Next, draw a 2 × 2 square on top of the first square. So if the first square was 0.5 cm, the 2 × 2 square should be 1 cm square, right? (Measure it with your ruler to make sure.)

10. Continue this pattern, making each square the next size in the Fibonacci sequence just as you did in the first exercise. After you draw the 2 × 2 square, you would make a 3 × 3 square (1.5 cm × 1.5 cm), then a 5 × 5 square (2.5 cm × 2.5 cm), and so on. Keep going until you have made a square that is 21 × 21 (10.5 cm × 10.5 cm).

    Each square will have an edge that is the sum of the two squares before it, just like in the Fibonacci sequence.

11. Using your compass, make an arc in the squares with a radius the size of the edge of the square. (This just means that the arc will be 1/4 of a circle.) The arcs in the first squares will be really, really tiny. But look how they grow! What does this remind you of?

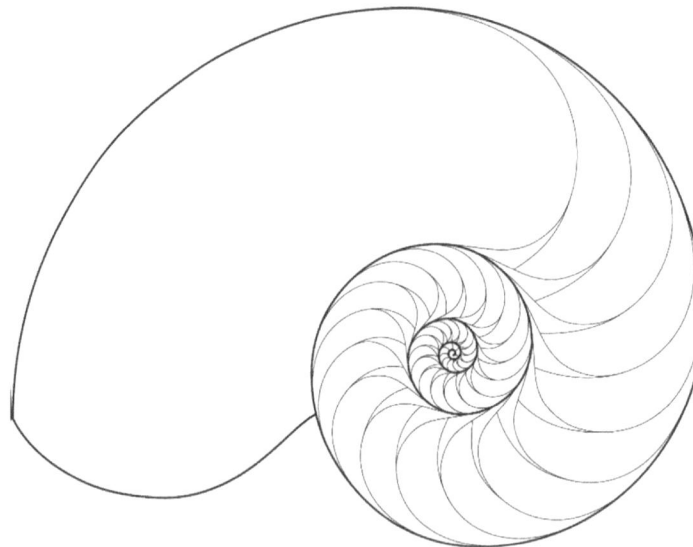

Assessment & Evaluation:

- Your student(s) can write the Fibonacci sequence.
- Your student(s) can identify Fibonacci numbers in nature and art.
- Your student(s) can create the Golden Rectangle.

Find us on f

Follow us on Facebook for more STEM/STEAM activities!

https://www.facebook.com/SteamTeam5/

Notes

www.ingramcontent.com/pod-product-compliance
Lightning Source LLC
LaVergne TN
LVHW072052070426

835508LV00002B/56